For Augustine Oti Yeboah and Mr Agri Pascal for your friendship and dedicated community conservation work with pangolins in Ghana.—CB

For my future grandchildren.—SW

For my niece Seren, with love.—AH

The publisher and authors would like to thank W.M. Adams, Emeritus Moran Professor of Conservation and Development, University of Cambridge and Chris Sandbrook, Professor of Conservation & Society, University of Cambridge for their invaluable expert advice.

First published in 2023 by Frances Lincoln Children's Books, an imprint of The Quarto Group.
100 Cummings Center, Suite 265D, Beverly, MA 01915, USA.
T +1 978-282-9590 F +1 078-283-2742 www.quarto.com

ISBN: 978-0-7112-7805-9
eISBN: 978-0-7112-7804-2

The illustrations were created digitally.
Set in Gill Sans.

Published by Peter Marley
Art directed by Karissa Santos
Designed by Holly Jolley
Edited by Claire Grace and Lotte Dobson
Production by Dawn Cameron

Manufactured in Guangdong, China TT042023
1 3 5 7 9 8 6 4 2

# The Story of
# CONSERVATION

## A first book about protecting nature

**Catherine Barr** and
**Steve Williams**
Illustrated by **Amy Husband**

Frances Lincoln
Children's Books

Long ago, our planet was blanketed with dark forests, dripping rainforests, frozen deserts, mighty mountains, sun-baked grasslands, and rich blue seas. Nature thrived in this prehistoric world.

The dinosaurs were long gone. Over time, humans became part of life on Earth and got their food from wild plants and animals. They painted their stories on cave walls: stories of battles between beasts and predators. These early people lived as part of nature.

# Some humans continued to gather and hunt for their food,

while others tamed and raised animals or grew plants. Around the world people changed the land around them in different ways. In some cultures, people became rich by trading crops and livestock.

There are fewer than last year.

In some places in Ancient Asia, traders picked wild mushrooms, looked for mussels, and trapped animals for fur. Some rulers saw nature shrinking and made laws to protect it—but usually to benefit wealthy and powerful people.

1600s–1830s

Driven by a hunger for land and wealth, powerful empires stole land and resources from communities around the world. They felled great forests for building, boats, and fuel.

The discovery of coal, oil, and gas changed the world. Burning these fossil fuels made new technologies possible, but demanded much more from nature. Cities spread as the Industrial Revolution swept the world.

Some people turned away from polluting cities to celebrate nature with art, poetry, and books. Others were eager to understand, study, organize, and collect nature. These naturalists learned from ancient science and shared exciting new discoveries about the natural world.

1800s

In places far from modern industry, Indigenous peoples lived in traditional ways, mostly without harming the natural world.

In North America, a landscape of rivers, eagles, wolves, and bears was cared for and respected by Indigenous peoples. But European settlers discovered the beauty and resources of this wild place and set out to claim it, pushing Indigenous peoples off the land.

Yellowstone became the world's first national park. The US government was persuaded to protect huge areas of land across the American West. Nature was protected but Indigenous peoples were removed from these lands. National parks soon sprang up everywhere: to protect Canadian mountains, New Zealand volcanoes, Swedish alpine glaciers, African forests, and Australian coral seas.

This idea of protecting nature spread... but the voices of Indigenous peoples were mostly ignored.

1870s–1900

In some parts of the world, humans consumed nature on an ever-grander scale. Women in Western cities wore feathers and even whole birds on their hats. Wealthy people became tourists and on safari in Africa and India they wanted trophies like elephant tusks and tiger skins.

In the American West, European pioneers boarded a new railway to hunt down millions of buffalo. Their arrival devastated communities who also relied on these majestic herds.

In a modernizing world, cities and farmland spread and great forests were felled. But early conservationists began to question this relentless destruction. They connected across continents to campaign for change.

1900s

Conservationists began to understand ecosystems.
They discovered how living things connect and what happens when just one species disappears. This helped people work out why nature was in trouble and sparked conversation about what must be done.

1935–1962

Scientists talked about fixing the problems that humans caused. They recorded, measured, and observed nature to find out more. The spotlight fell on farming. In North America, a scientist called Rachel Carson studied chemicals used on crops to kill pests. These deadly crop sprays were poisoning birds, other wildlife, and potentially even people too. In a bestselling book, she explained how nature works and why, without birds, the world risked falling silent in spring.

New technologies helped people understand nature like never before. Some zoomed in on minute details, others focused on a much bigger picture. In the silence of space and quiet of the deep sea, explorers revealed new ways of looking at planet Earth.

This will make a great photo!

1960s

As the pioneering Apollo 8 spacecraft curved around the moon, astronauts saw a brilliant blue marble rising out of inky blackness. They stared at Earth swirling with clouds, oceans, light, and life.

Back on our blue planet, scientists dived down in a submersible to explore the ocean floor. Pictures of strange creatures, fiery underwater volcanoes, and a photograph of our blue dot in space inspired wonder that transformed people's view of life on Earth.

Despite having a better understanding of nature, humans continued to damage our world. People rose up in protest to save Earth. They made films, took photographs, painted banners, and shared science. This environmental movement urged everyone, everywhere, to take it personally, be bold, and get involved!

Deforestation in the mountains of the Himalayas was protested against by the Chipko movement, where a group of women joined hands to hug trees, inspiring people around the world to save forests big and small. Air pollution burned a hole in Earth's atmosphere, letting in the sun's most dangerous rays... until world leaders were persuaded to ban chemicals causing this pollution. These stories and many, many more spread across the world and inspired others to take a stand.

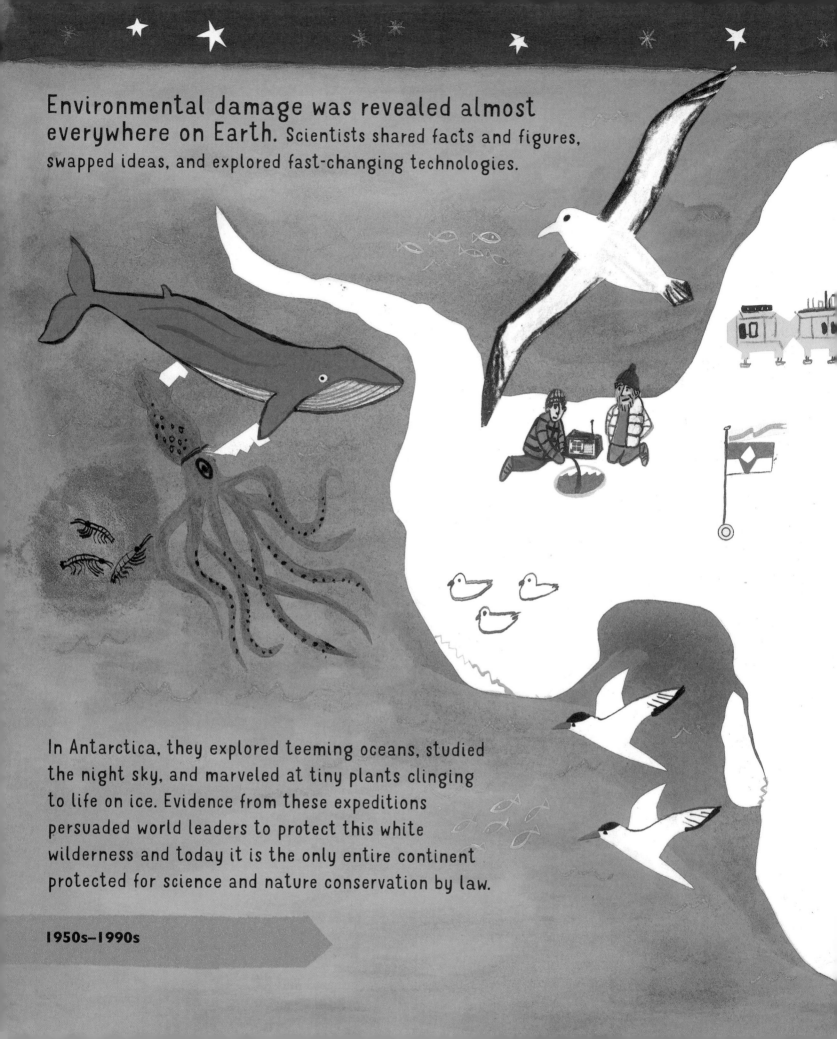

Environmental damage was revealed almost everywhere on Earth. Scientists shared facts and figures, swapped ideas, and explored fast-changing technologies.

In Antarctica, they explored teeming oceans, studied the night sky, and marveled at tiny plants clinging to life on ice. Evidence from these expeditions persuaded world leaders to protect this white wilderness and today it is the only entire continent protected for science and nature conservation by law.

**1950s–1990s**

Technology improved and space satellites began recording changes in nature on land as well as monitoring weather. The internet helped people share images, data, and news. With better information, conservationists could make better plans to protect both habitats and species.

Scientists became increasingly alarmed by pollution from burning fossil fuels. The pollution was driving climate change, which was driving changing patterns of rain, wildfires, floods, storms, and rising seas. Together they warned that humans must end this pollution to save the world.

Climate change is powered by rich countries, where people use more energy and more stuff. This demand is destroying nature everywhere. Rainforests are felled for timber, meat, soy, and palm oil. Deserts are spreading as less rain falls, crops fail, and habitats shift.

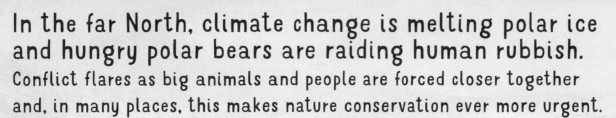

In the far North, climate change is melting polar ice and hungry polar bears are raiding human rubbish. Conflict flares as big animals and people are forced closer together and, in many places, this makes nature conservation ever more urgent.

The Arctic National Wildlife Refuge, which is protected for its untouched beauty, is home to the Gwich'in and Iñupiat, Indigenous peoples of Alaska. But the Arctic shoreline is unprotected and this is where companies want oil deep under the ice. Yet these remote shores are vital for local fishing and caribou calving.

Facing this challenge, Alaska Natives met Indigenous leaders from Canada, Inuit from Greenland and Saami people from Europe and all shared similar stories. Across the planet, Indigenous peoples are demanding their right to live gently on sacred land.

On the Pacific islands of Palau, scientists and fisherfolk share ancient wisdom and scientific knowledge, learning how conservation works best. These fishing communities are living with climate change and, as polar ice melts, islands like Palau are in danger of flooding.

2017

On these remote islands, families make a living mostly from tourism and fishing. But as the numbers of tourists rose, the numbers of fish fell. Working alongside scientists, fisherfolk stopped fishing where stocks were low and over time sea-life returned and coral bloomed!

Far from tourist hot spots, some people hunt wild animals to eat and sell. But eating "wild-caught meat" has spiraled out of control. Driven by local poverty as well as urban demand, the wild-caught meat trade is threatening endangered species like pangolins, bonobos, and crocodiles, with extinction.

Can we go to the forest?

Today

In Ghana, some communities are keeping snails, rabbits, and bees for honey instead of hunting for food. Wildlife rangers use camera traps to collect information and help children to understand the role of pangolins in nature. All over the world, community projects like this are sharing knowledge, celebrating success, and changing minds.

All species have an important role to play and without diversity in nature, both people and wildlife are in trouble. In forest ecosystems, pangolins keep termites in check, bonobos are forest gardeners dispersing seeds in their poop, and crocodiles are important predators in the freshwater food chain.

Destruction of nature is often driven by greed but conservation costs money. From protecting one rare species to restoring a landscape, caring for nature involves difficult decisions about where and what to save.

Wild places are becoming isolated islands and these islands must connect for nature to thrive. Big animals like tigers, wolves, and elephants need room to roam. Migrating birds crossing continents need wetlands to rest, and in urban landscapes, pollinators like bees need flowers to feed.

But people have found many ways to conserve and celebrate nature. In the Norwegian capital of Oslo, bee-friendly flowers in gardens, on rooftops, and on windowsills create a colorful pollinator pathway across the city.

All over the world, when people take only what they need, nature blooms. Barren seas refill with fish, forests regrow, wildlife returns, and ecosystems flourish.

The most urgent challenge is to live in harmony with the natural world—and everyone, everywhere, is involved. People in richer countries must stop driving climate change. People in poverty must be heard. People in power must lead decisions that benefit nature and people. Consumers must live more sustainable lives...

**Today**

Are you ready to join in? Ask questions, make choices that support nature, and challenge people who do not. Everything you do matters. Together, let's be bold enough to save our wild and wonderful world.

Ready for action?

Stand up for nature!

# Glossary of useful words

**Climate change**—long-term changes in the world's climate. Today it is mostly caused by people burning fossil fuels as well as large-scale deforestation.

**Conservation**—looking after and protecting living things and the places they live in.

**Deforestation**—cutting down trees for wood, building, farming, or mining.

**Empire**—a group of countries living under one ruler.

**Endangered**—a living thing threatened with extinction.

**Environmental movement**—groups of people working together to protect the environment.

**Extinction**—the disappearance of all individuals of one type of living thing.

**Fossil fuels**—natural fuels made of fossilized plants and animals, for example, coal, oil, and gas.

**Indigenous peoples**—people who have always lived in a place.

**Industrial Revolution**—the period of time when work began to be done by more steam-powered machines in factories and the mass production of goods.

**National Park**—a wild area of land protected by law.

**Prehistoric**—a time before records were written down by humans.

**Sacred**—something that deserves respect, usually linked to religion.

**Settlers**—people who move to live in another place.

**Submersible**—a vehicle that people use to work underwater.

**Sustainable**—a way of using nature that causes little or no damage to the environment.

**Technologies**—the use of scientific discoveries to solve problems.

**Trophies**—dead animals or parts of animals that are used to show off hunting skills or used for decoration.